Autumn
Leaves

Autu

Le

mn

by Ken Robbins

aves

SCHOLASTIC INC.
New York Toronto London Auckland Sydney
Mexico City New Delhi Hong Kong

All the featured leaves in this book are shown at life-size.

ISBN 0-439-14988-6

12 11 10 9 8 7 6 5 4 3 2 1   9/9 0 1 2 3 4/0

Printed in the U.S.A.   14

First Scholastic club printing, September 1999

Book design by Ken Robbins and Becky Terhune
The text is set in 20-point Bauer Bodoni.

Facing page: *cut leaf maple*

For Maria

*A*utumn is a time to look closely at leaves. In spring and summer the leaves on most trees are green. But in autumn those green leaves turn different colors and fall to the ground. Some leaves just dry up and turn a dull brown, while others turn colors that are brilliant and bold: orange, yellow, red, purple, and gold, painting the landscape and changing the world.

birch

The leaves of most trees are flat and thin. Most are connected to the tree by a stem.

norway maple

All leaves have veins. The veins of some leaves are quite easy to see.

sweet chestnut

Some leaves are shiny, some are dull.

Some have shapes that are simple.

smoke tree

Some have shapes that are not.

red oak

Sometimes lots of leaflets make up a leaf.

honey locust

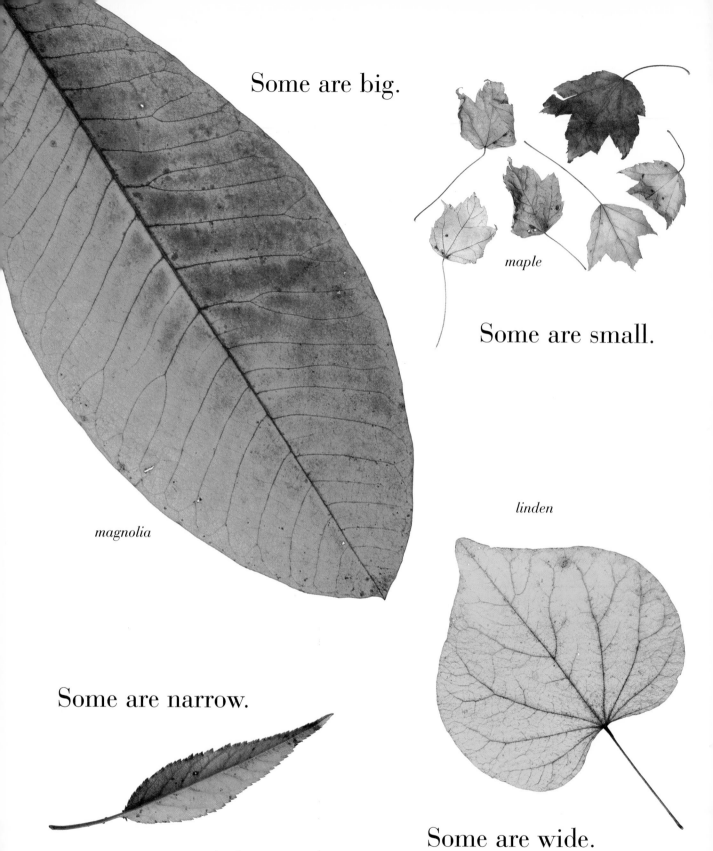

Some are big.

maple

Some are small.

magnolia

linden

Some are narrow.

Some are wide.

pin cherry

sassafras

Some leaves are not the same on their right and left sides.

aspen

Others have edges that are jagged,

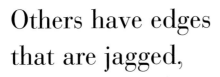

or edges that are smooth.

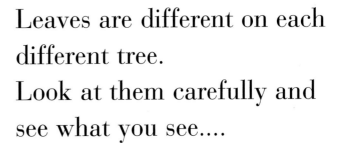

sourwood

Leaves are different on each different tree.
Look at them carefully and see what you see....

Smoke Tree

The smoke tree's leaves are shaped like paddles.
The stalks of its flowers are so thin and fine
that from a distance they look like smoke.

Birch

The bark of the gray birch is white and smooth,
and shines like silver when it catches the light.
Birch leaves have jagged edges.

Gingko

Gingko trees grew in prehistoric times.
Dinosaurs once ate their fan-shaped leaves.

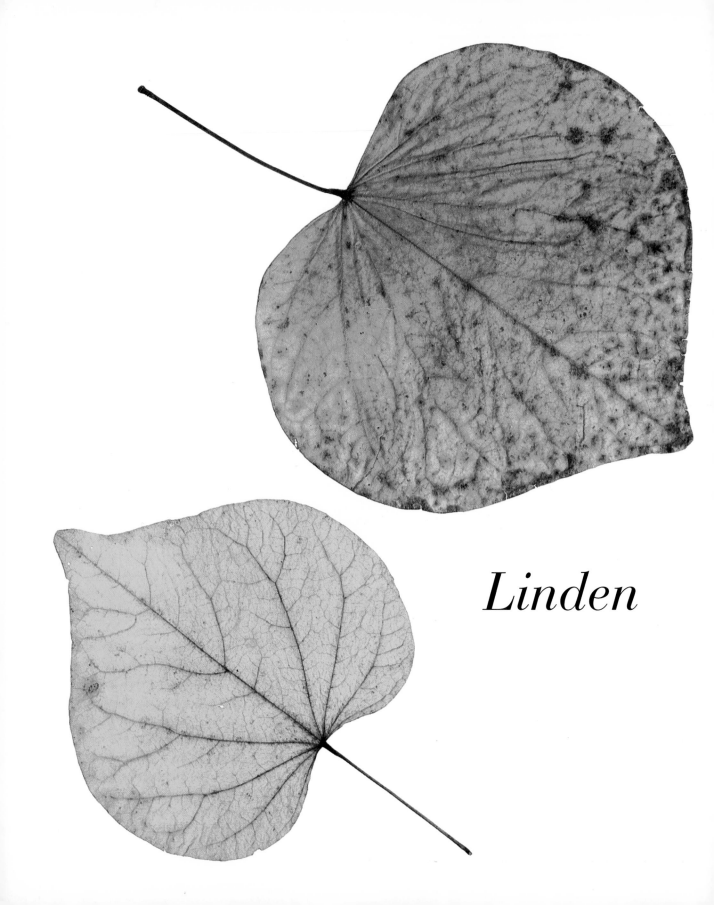

Linden

The leaves of the linden tree are rather large, and shaped like hearts.

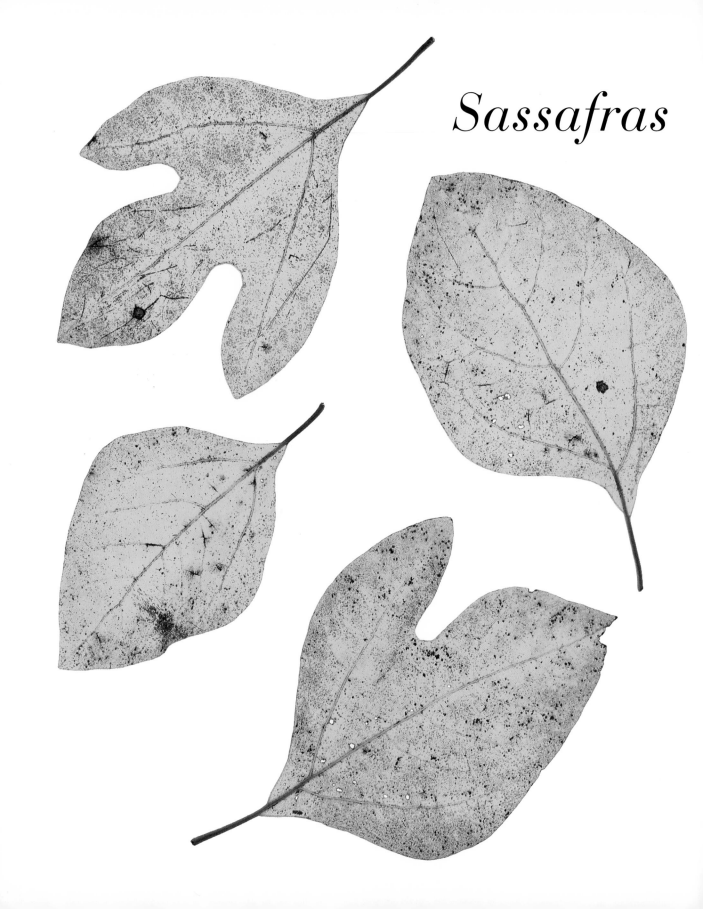

Sassafras

Several different shapes of leaves can grow
on the branches of one sassafras tree.
Some even look like mittens.

Sweet Gum

The leaves of the sweet gum tree are almost always shaped like stars.

Hickory

There are compound leaves on the hickory tree.
Five leaflets or more make up the leaf.

Red Oak

Red oak trees have pointed leaves.
Oak trees come in many different forms,
but they all make acorns in the fall.

Fern Leaf
Beech

The fern leaf beech has smooth, gray bark.
Its leaves, when they're dry, look like
question marks.

Cherry

Cherries are the fruit of the cherry tree.
Some are sour, some are sweet.
Cherry tree leaves are shinier on one
side than they are on the other.

Dogwood

The dogwood tree has beautiful flowers in the
early spring. The pretty dogwood leaves
are like ovals with points.

*Yellow
Poplar*

The yellow poplar is also called the tulip tree.
The leaves look a little like a tulip flower.

Maple

Maples trees often have the brightest and
most colorful leaves of all the trees in the fall.

Green leaves make food out of something as slight
As carbon dioxide and water and light.

Green leaves make a kind of sugar to help trees grow. It's made from water and light and a part of the air called carbon dioxide. There is a proper word for this: photosynthesis. There are special scientific words for the chemicals that give leaves their color: it's chlorophyll that makes them green; the yellow is from xanthophyll; the orange is carotene. The reds and purples are anthocyanin, and brown is the result of something called tannin.

When photosynthesis stops in fall, the green part of leaves dries up and dies. Then we start to see the amazing colors, the yellows and golds, that were there all the time. And sometimes a bit of sugar gets left in the leaf when it dies; that turns the leaf purple or red for a while. Sooner or later all those colors fade to brown.

Eventually, the base of the stem, where the leaf is attached to the tree, grows brittle. Then when the wind blows even a little, the leaf breaks off and flutters through the air to the ground, and before you know it all the leaves are down and the trees are bare.